Y0-BZE-394

LOS ANGELES RAMS

BY WILLIAM MEIER

SportsZone
An Imprint of Abdo Publishing
abdobooks.com

abdobooks.com

Published by Abdo Publishing, a division of ABDO, PO Box 398166, Minneapolis, Minnesota 55439.

Printed in the United States of America, North Mankato, Minnesota
042019
092019

Cover Photo: Kyusung Gong/AP Images
Interior Photos: NFL Photos/AP Images, 5, 7, 14, 17, 18, 23, 25, 31, 43; John Gaps III/AP Images, 9; AP Images, 11, 12, 27; Vic Stein/Getty Images Sport/Getty Images, 21; Owen C. Shaw/Getty Images Sport/Getty Images, 29; James A. Finley/AP Images, 32; Tom Gannam/AP Images, 35; Mike McCarn/AP Images, 37; Greg Trott/AP Images, 38; Margaret Bowles/AP Images, 41

Editor: Patrick Donnelly
Series Designer: Craig Hinton

Library of Congress Control Number: 2018965653

Publisher's Cataloging-in-Publication Data

Names: Meier, William, author.
Title: Los Angeles Rams / by William Meier
Description: Minneapolis, Minnesota: Abdo Publishing, 2020 | Series: Inside the NFL | Includes online resources and index.
Identifiers: ISBN 9781532118548 (lib. bdg.) | ISBN 9781532172724 (ebook) | ISBN 9781644941096 (pbk.)
Subjects: LCSH: Los Angeles Rams (Football team : 2016-)--Juvenile literature. | National Football League--Juvenile literature. | Football teams--Juvenile literature. | American football--Juvenile literature.
Classification: DDC 796.33264--dc23

TABLE OF CONTENTS

CHAPTER 1

THE GREATEST SHOW ON TURF

Things were looking up for the 1999 St. Louis Rams. The team had a great coach in Dick Vermeil, a star running back in Marshall Faulk, and a hometown quarterback in Trent Green.

But suddenly, that all seemed to fall apart. In the Rams' third preseason game, Green suffered a season-ending knee injury. Vermeil had to turn to little-known backup Kurt Warner to run the offense.

Just a few years earlier, Warner was stocking shelves at a grocery store. He had played college football but had never started an NFL game. That made what he did in 1999 even more incredible.

Warner was an immediate success as a starter. He threw three touchdown passes in each of his first three starts—an

Rams running back Marshall Faulk looks for space to run in Super Bowl XXXIV.

RAMS
28

RECORD BREAKER

Marshall Faulk quickly fit in with the Rams. In 1999 he totaled 2,429 yards of total offense, setting an NFL record at the time, while also scoring 12 touchdowns. That broke Detroit Lions legend Barry Sanders's record of 2,358 all-purpose yards set in 1997. Faulk had 1,381 rushing yards (averaging 5.5 yards per carry) and 1,048 receiving yards (12.0 yards per catch).

Faulk is the only player with at least 12,000 rushing yards and 6,000 receiving yards in his career. Among his other unmatched feats are seven two-point conversions, five games of 250-plus yards from scrimmage, and 14 games of 200-plus yards from scrimmage. He is also the only player to record at least 70 rushing touchdowns and 30 or more receiving touchdowns. Faulk retired in 2007 after missing the 2006 season with injuries. He was inducted into the Pro Football Hall of Fame in 2011.

NFL first. Then in his fourth game, against the San Francisco 49ers, Warner threw a touchdown pass on each of the Rams' first three possessions. He finished the game with five touchdown passes.

Warner, Faulk, wide receivers Isaac Bruce and Torry Holt, and the rest of the St. Louis offense became known as the "Greatest Show on Turf." The artificial turf at their home stadium, the Edward Jones Dome, helped showcase their quickness and speed.

Meanwhile, Warner went on to have one of the best statistical seasons a quarterback has ever turned in. He won

Rams quarterback Kurt Warner rolls out of the pocket in search of a receiver in Super Bowl XXXIV.

the NFL's Most Valuable Player (MVP) Award after completing 65.1 percent of his passes for 4,353 yards and 41 touchdowns. The Rams finished 13–3 while scoring an amazing 526 points

(32.9 per game). They rode that red-hot offense all the way to the Super Bowl.

The Rams' dramatic season continued until the very last play of the Super Bowl against the Tennessee Titans. At the Georgia Dome in Atlanta, the Rams took a 16–0 lead in the third quarter. But Tennessee began to fight back. Titans running back Eddie George scored two touchdowns. Their two-point conversion after the first touchdown failed. But they added a field goal to tie the game with only 2:12 left.

With momentum now firmly on the Titans' side, Warner and the Rams offense trotted onto the field. On the first play of the drive, the NFL MVP hit Bruce for a 73-yard touchdown strike. The Rams took a 23–16 lead.

The Titans did not quit. They got the ball back with 1:48 left and drove down the field. With six seconds left, Tennessee had the ball on the Rams' 10-yard line. The final

SEE YA, KURT

Kurt Warner finally retired after the 2009 season. He was 38 years old. Upon being released by the Rams after the 2003 season, Warner joined the New York Giants and then the Arizona Cardinals. After the 2008 season, Warner led the Cardinals to their first Super Bowl. He finished his career with 32,344 passing yards and 208 touchdown passes. He was inducted into the Pro Football Hall of Fame in 2017.

Rams linebacker Mike Jones wraps up Titans receiver Kevin Dyson, keeping him out of the end zone at the end of Super Bowl XXXIV.

play of Super Bowl XXXIV was one of the most dramatic plays in NFL history.

The Titans needed to score on this final play in order to tie the game. Tennessee quarterback Steve McNair took the snap and dropped back to find a receiver. He quickly spotted wide receiver Kevin Dyson cutting across the field from his right. Dyson caught the ball on the run near the 5-yard line. As he turned and tried to force his way into the end zone, Rams linebacker Mike Jones wrapped him up. Dyson stretched, but he couldn't quite reach the goal line. The Greatest Show on Turf had finally brought a Super Bowl to the Rams franchise and to St. Louis.

CHAPTER 2

CLEVELAND ROOTS

In February 1937 the NFL granted a team to Homer Marshman and Associates for $10,000. The group of businessmen from Cleveland, Ohio, became the first owners of the Rams. Marshman, an attorney, adopted the Rams nickname because his general manager, Buzz Wetzel, was a fan of the Fordham University Rams. Marshman liked how the name "Rams" sounded.

Hugo Bezdek was hired as the Rams' first coach. The team's first game was against the Detroit Lions at Cleveland's Municipal Stadium on September 10, 1937. The Lions won 28–0. The first Rams team finished just 1–10.

In 1939 Dutch Clark took over as the Rams' coach. Clark had been a star running back for the Lions from 1934 to 1938.

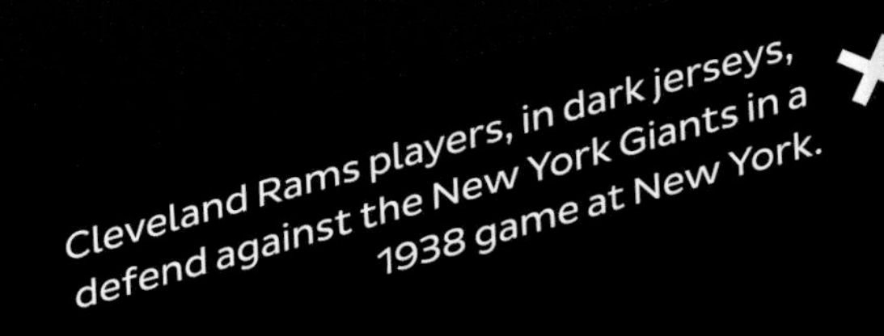

Cleveland Rams players, in dark jerseys, defend against the New York Giants in a 1938 game at New York.

26
36
13

From left, Corby Davis, Rudy Mucha, Johnny Drake, and Parker Hall pose for a photo in 1941.

He also coached them in his last two seasons as a player. In Clark's first year, the Rams improved to 5–5–1. But that was the team's best record during this period.

Things started to look up beginning with the 1944 draft. In the fifth round, the Rams picked quarterback Bob Waterfield from the University of California, Los Angeles (UCLA). He returned from military service and joined the Rams for the 1945 season. Waterfield quickly meshed with his new teammates.

EARNING HIS PAY

Bob Waterfield's championship-season play in 1945 earned him the richest contract in the NFL at the time. Owner Dan Reeves , who had purchased the team in 1941, gave Waterfield $60,000 for three years, beginning with the 1946 season.

Waterfield earned his pay. Nicknamed "The Rifle" for his strong arm, he also doubled as a defensive back his first four seasons, intercepting 20 passes. During the middle part of the century, quarterbacks often handled place-kicking and punting duties. Waterfield kicked 60 field goals during his career and booted more than 300 extra points. He retired after the 1952 season and was inducted into the Pro Football Hall of Fame in 1965.

Coach Adam Walsh guided his more talented team to a 4–0 start in 1945. The Rams finished the regular season 9–1. In the NFL Championship Game, they faced Washington on December 16 in a snow-filled Municipal Stadium. The day was so cold—just 2 degrees Fahrenheit (minus-17°C)—that players covered themselves in hay while on the sidelines to keep warm.

A crowd of 32,178 fans showed up for the game. The Rams fans who braved the chill got to see Waterfield throw a 37-yard pass to Jim Benton for a touchdown. He also threw a 44-yard pass to running back Jim Gillette for another score. The Rams then held on for a tight 15–14 victory and an NFL title. Little did the fans know it would their last chance to root for the hometown team.

Los Angeles Rams running back Fred Gehrke was responsible for painting the trademark horns on the Rams helmet.

Citing poor attendance, Rams owner Dan Reeves announced the team's move to Los Angeles just one month after the NFL Championship Game. The Rams would be the first major league sports team to play on the west coast. They would play home games in the 100,000-seat Los Angeles Memorial Coliseum. The massive stadium had hosted the 1932 Summer Olympics.

THE CLEVELAND BROWNS

Many people believed that Paul Brown would take over as the Rams' coach after the 1945 season. He was already a successful high school coach in Ohio and had also led Ohio State University to the 1942 national title. Instead, Rams owner Dan Reeves moved the team to California, and Brown helped found a team in the new All-America Football Conference (AAFC). In 1950 the Cleveland Browns joined the NFL. After spending 50 seasons in a rapidly deteriorating Municipal Stadium, the team moved to Baltimore and became the Ravens before the 1996 season. However, the NFL immediately awarded an expansion team to Cleveland that would begin play in 1999 in a new stadium. The new team assumed the Browns' name, colors, and history.

Although the Coliseum offered seemingly unlimited seating capacity, the team faced challenges out west. In 1946 the closest city with an NFL team was Chicago, more than 2,000 miles (3,200 km) away. Travel was time-consuming. Cross-country trains took two or three days. Propeller-driven airplanes—half as fast as modern jets—used up most of one day and usually required a stop or two to get to the East Coast. To solve the problem, Reeves offered $5,000 to opponents who would play the Rams in Los Angeles.

The Rams became innovators in other ways, as well. In 1934 NFL owners began signing only white players to contracts. But in 1946, Reeves signed running back Kenny Washington and receiver Woody Strode. They were the first black players

"CRAZYLEGS" HIRSCH

Elroy "Crazylegs" Hirsch got his nickname for his zigzag running style while playing college football. The Rams drafted Hirsch in 1945, but he played his first three seasons with the AAFC's Chicago Rockets. He was a running back when he first came to the Rams. Then he became a full-time wide receiver just in time for the title run in 1951. "Crazylegs" became known for catching long passes with his fingertips while on the run. They became known as "Elroy Hirsch Specials."

Hirsch stayed on with the Rams after his retirement in 1957. He was the team's general manager from 1960 to 1969. Hirsch then went back to his home state of Wisconsin, where he served as the athletic director at the University of Wisconsin.

in the NFL since the informal ban had been implemented 12 years earlier. One year later, Jackie Robinson broke the color barrier in Major League Baseball with the Brooklyn Dodgers.

Reeves did not stop with Washington and Strode. The Rams became pro sports' most integrated team. They soon added running backs "Deacon Dan" Towler and Tank Younger, along with defensive stars Bob Boyd and Dick "Night Train" Lane. Towler and Younger teamed with Dick Hoerner to form the "Bull Elephant" backfield. Each player weighed at least 225 pounds—which in those days was about the size of an average lineman.

Meanwhile, the team added star receivers Elroy "Crazylegs" Hirsch and Tom Fears as targets

Elroy "Crazylegs" Hirsch was known for his ability to catch long passes.

for Waterfield's passes. Coach Clark Shaughnessy guided the team to the Western Division title in 1949. However, the Rams lost 14–0 to the Philadelphia Eagles in the NFL Championship Game. Former Bears lineman Joe Stydahar replaced Shaughnessy as head coach in 1950. But the Rams were frustrated again in the NFL Championship Game. They lost

Quarterback Bob Waterfield guided the Rams' feared offense from 1945 to 1952.

30–28 to the Cleveland Browns, the team that began playing at Municipal Stadium immediately after the Rams moved west.

The Rams were football's top offensive team in 1950. They even scored 70 points in one game. And they used two quarterbacks to do it. The Rams drafted Norm Van Brocklin out of the University of Oregon in 1949. When he began splitting time with Waterfield in 1950, the duo put up huge numbers. In the 1951 season opener, Van Brocklin threw for 554 yards against the now-defunct New York Yanks. Through 2018 that remained an NFL record for most passing yards in a game.

Waterfield was an effective player, but he truly thrived with Van Brocklin's help. Complementing each other, the quarterbacks helped lead the Rams to an 8–4 regular season. Waterfield and Van Brocklin each threw 13 touchdown passes. Hirsch gained 1,495 receiving yards while Fears, who had caught 18 passes in one game a year earlier, remained a threat.

On December 23, 1951, the Rams met the Browns again in the NFL Championship Game. Although the Rams' offense was considered the league's best, the Browns and their own star signal caller, Otto Graham, were not far behind.

More than 59,000 fans showed up at the Coliseum to see the rematch. The three star quarterbacks were largely held in check throughout the game. But the Rams made a big play midway through the fourth quarter. Van Brocklin hit Fears for a 73-yard touchdown pass that broke a 17–17 tie. As the clock ticked to zero, hundreds of Rams fans stormed onto the field to celebrate with their heroes. With a 24–17 win, the Rams had won their first NFL Championship since moving to Los Angeles.

CHAPTER 3

FALLING SHORT

The Rams continued to be high-scoring title contenders for the first half of the 1950s. Under coach Sid Gillman, they made the 1955 NFL Championship Game. But they lost 38–14 to the Cleveland Browns. After that, the Rams began a long decline. They lost more games than they won in nine of the next 10 seasons.

Although the Rams were not successful on the field, they remained popular in Los Angeles. The team drew 102,368 fans, then an NFL record, to one game in 1957. They averaged 74,296 fans per game that year.

A familiar face took over as coach in 1960. It was former Rams quarterback Bob Waterfield. But Waterfield could not guide his old team to a winning season.

Roman Gabriel was the Rams' quarterback throughout most of the 1960s.

ROMAN GABRIEL

Rams quarterback Roman Gabriel threw 25 touchdown passes in 1967 and 24 in 1969. Gabriel helped make the Rams one of the strongest teams in the NFL with 11 wins in both seasons. But he did not have his greatest overall season until he was traded to the Philadelphia Eagles in 1973. That year Gabriel threw for a personal-best 3,219 yards.

In the NFL, the teams with the worst records get the highest draft picks. In 1962 the Rams picked defensive tackle Merlin Olsen and quarterback Roman Gabriel in the first round. They joined linemen David "Deacon" Jones and Lamar Lundy as young stars on the squad. Defensive tackle Rosey Grier came over from the New York Giants in 1963.

The building blocks for a successful team were in place. In 1966 Rams owner Dan Reeves hired George Allen to take over as head coach. Allen had been the defensive coordinator of the Chicago Bears. The Olsen-Jones-Lundy-Grier defensive line soon became known as "the Fearsome Foursome." They fronted a strong, all-veteran defense. Allen had little tolerance for rookies, who took more time to develop.

Allen surrounded Gabriel with veteran offensive linemen. He also had wide receiver Jack Snow to work with. The 1966 Rams finished 8–6. Many fans expected the team to take a big step forward the next season. And they did. The 1967 Rams

From left, the "Fearsome Foursome" of Merlin Olsen, Lamar Lundy, Deacon Jones, and Roger Brown close in on the Colts in 1967.

became a dominant team, finishing 11–1–2. However, they drew a tough matchup in the playoffs. The Green Bay Packers were nearing the end of their famed dynasty. But they were still powerful enough to beat the Rams 28–7.

The Rams won 30 games from 1968 to 1970 under Allen. But they made the playoffs just once. They lost to the Minnesota Vikings in 1969. Allen was fired after a second-place finish in 1970, but new head coach Tommy Prothro didn't do much better in his two years at the helm.

FEARSOME LONGEVITY

The Fearsome Foursome only underwent one change in the '60s. Roger Brown replaced Rosey Grier, who was forced into retirement by a ruptured Achilles tendon.

New owner Carroll Rosenbloom hired Chuck Knox as coach for the 1973 season. He also added veteran John Hadl at quarterback, while running back Lawrence McCutcheon began a five-year streak in which he averaged more than 1,100 rushing yards per season. The Rams were again dominant in the regular season, finishing 12–2. It was the first of seven straight National Football Conference (NFC) West titles for the Rams. But falling short in the playoffs would continue to be a theme. In 1973 they lost to the Dallas Cowboys in the first round 27–16.

In 1974 quarterback James Harris became the first black quarterback to start regularly in the NFL. He led the Rams to their first playoff victory since 1951, beating Washington 19–10. But the Rams fell short in their bid to reach their first Super Bowl. They lost to the Minnesota Vikings 14–10 in the NFC Championship Game.

Knox and the Rams continued to be frustrated, losing in the NFC Championship Game in 1975 and again in 1976. A divisional-round loss to the Vikings in 1977 led to Knox's dismissal. Ray Malavasi took over as head coach in 1978 and

Rams running back Lawrence McCutcheon (30) and quarterback James Harris celebrate a McCutcheon touchdown in 1975.

took the Rams back to the NFC title game—where they lost to the Cowboys, 28–0. But 1979 would turn out to be perhaps the strangest year in Rams history. It also produced their first trip to the Super Bowl—and an ultimate near miss.

Tragedy struck the Rams even before the 1979 season began. On April 2, Rosenbloom died in a drowning accident.

GEORGE ALLEN

George Allen had a strange, three-part coaching career with the Rams. He was first offered the job in 1966. It was common for teams to allow an assistant to break a contract for a head coaching job. However, the Chicago Bears would not let him break his contract as an assistant coach. The Bears sued Allen before finally releasing him.

After three seasons with the Rams, Allen had conflicts with team owner Dan Reeves and was fired. But fans picketed the Rams' office, and 7,500 signed a petition to bring him back. He was rehired in January but fired again after two seasons. Allen was rehired again after the 1977 season. New owner Carroll Rosenbloom soon regretted that decision. Allen preferred veterans, so he began getting rid of the team's young, talented players. He was fired for the third time after two preseason games in 1978.

Then their quarterbacks began dropping. Starter Pat Haden suffered a broken finger in November. Backup Bob Lee was injured in his second game. The Rams were forced to turn to third-stringer Vince Ferragamo. They still won five of their final seven games to finish 9–7 and sneak into the playoffs. There, they upset the Cowboys 21–19. Then Los Angeles edged out the Tampa Bay Buccaneers 9–0 in the NFC Championship Game. They would face the three-time champion Pittsburgh Steelers at Super Bowl XIV.

The Rams played the big game close to home in front of their own fans. More than 103,000 people crammed into the Rose Bowl in nearby Pasadena, California, on January 20, 1980.

The Rams offense huddles during Super Bowl XIV. They lost to the Pittsburgh Steelers 31–19.

The Rams led 13–10 at halftime. McCutcheon threw a 24-yard touchdown pass to Ron Smith on a trick play. That gave Los Angeles a 19–17 lead going into the fourth quarter. But Pittsburgh's star quarterback Terry Bradshaw tossed a 73-yard touchdown pass to John Stallworth to give the Steelers the lead. Running back Franco Harris scored an insurance touchdown, and the Steelers won 31–19.

"There was no loser today," Bradshaw said. "Both teams deserved the title. The Rams are one tough club." But such small consolations were all the Rams could cling to for another two decades.

CHAPTER 4

BIG NAMES, BUT NO BIG PRIZE

The Rams' Cinderella season in 1979 had just a short carryover. The team moved down the freeway to Anaheim Stadium for the 1980 season. They finished 11–5 but once again made a quick exit from the playoffs.

Star running back Eric Dickerson soon ushered in a new era of greatness. Between 1984 and 1989, the Rams won either 10 or 11 games in five seasons. Dickerson had become the NFL's top running back immediately after he was drafted in the first round in 1983. He gained a league-leading 1,808 yards in his rookie season. Then he really stepped on the gas in the 1984 season.

Dickerson rushed for an NFL-record 2,105 yards. He averaged 131.6 yards per game and 5.6 yards per carry

Quarterback Jim Everett drops back to pass in a 1988 game at Anaheim Stadium.

11

A RUNNER FIRST

Eric Dickerson was one of the top running backs of all time. Unlike many running backs of his era, however, Dickerson wasn't a big part of the team's passing game. Dickerson caught 51 passes his rookie year in 1983. But then he never snared more than 26 in any of his other three full seasons as a Ram. Dickerson was inducted into the Pro Football Hall of Fame in 1999.

that year. Dickerson broke the NFL single-season record of 2,003 rushing yards set by O. J. Simpson of the Buffalo Bills in 1973. But by 1987, Dickerson had become dissatisfied with his contract. He demanded a trade and was dealt to the Indianapolis Colts in the middle of that season.

Quarterback Jim Everett then became the face of the Rams. He led the NFL with 31 touchdown passes in 1988. Receiver Henry Ellard was a favorite target. Running back Greg Bell, whom the Rams got in the Dickerson trade, became a big contributor. He had 1,212 rushing yards and an NFL-leading 16 rushing touchdowns. The Rams had one more solid regular season but then began to decline.

During all of those successful seasons, the Rams made it to the NFC Championship Game just twice. They lost to the Chicago Bears 24–0 in January 1986. Then they lost to their archrival, the San Francisco 49ers, 30–3 in January 1990. Once again, a Super Bowl championship was frustratingly elusive.

Rams running back Eric Dickerson finds space to run during a 1986 win over the Atlanta Falcons.

As the Rams declined, attendance in Anaheim dropped, too. Owner Georgia Frontiere, who had taken over the team after husband Carroll Rosenbloom died, was unable to get a new stadium built in the area. So she looked to her hometown of St. Louis, Missouri, for a possible new home for the Rams. A domed stadium with all the modern amenities the Rams cherished was under construction in downtown St. Louis. So a deal was struck. After 49 years in the Los Angeles area, the Rams moved to St. Louis in 1995.

While construction finished on the dome, the Rams temporarily played in Busch Stadium, home of the St. Louis

Rams wide receiver Torry Holt celebrates after scoring a touchdown in 1999.

Cardinals baseball team. It also had hosted the NFL's Cardinals, who moved to Arizona in 1998. The Trans World Dome opened on November 12, 1995. The Rams defeated the Carolina Panthers 28–17 in their first game. It was the highlight of an otherwise forgettable 7–9 season.

But after a bumpy start, much better days were just a few years away. The arrival of Kurt Warner and the emergence of the "Greatest Show on Turf" made the Rams one of the most feared teams in the NFL.

Their success did not stop after the victory in Super Bowl XXXIV. Head coach Dick Vermeil retired after the 1999 season and was replaced by offensive coordinator Mike Martz. Under Martz the team's prolific offense upped its 1999 total by scoring 540 points in 2000. However, injuries slowed the team down. They finished 10–6 and lost in the first round of the playoffs.

ORLANDO PACE

In 1997 the Rams selected Ohio State University offensive tackle Orlando Pace with the first overall pick of the NFL Draft. The seven-time Pro Bowler became one of the top offensive linemen in the game. He also played a big part in helping the Rams reach two Super Bowls. He was inducted into the Pro Football Hall of Fame in 2016.

But they were back in 2001. Warner led the Rams to a 14–2 regular-season record. He also won his second NFL MVP Award, while Faulk was named the NFL Offensive Player of the Year. After winning two playoff games, the Rams faced the upstart New England Patriots in Super Bowl XXXVI.

Like the Rams' previous Super Bowl appearance, this one came down to the final play. But this time it did not go the Rams' way. Patriots kicker Adam Vinatieri made a field goal as time expired. The Patriots won 20–17 in what was considered a big upset. That three-year stretch from 1999 to 2001 was the high point of the team's relatively brief stay in St. Louis.

CHAPTER 5

GOING BACK TO CALIFORNIA

Despite having some talented offensive players, the Rams were unable to recapture the dominant form they displayed from 1999 to 2001. As the stars from their heyday began retiring or moving to other teams, the Rams struggled to replace them through the draft and free agency. From 2002 through 2016, the Rams had only one winning season. In 2009 they finished a league-worst 1–15 and barely resembled the team that had won the Super Bowl 10 years before.

The struggles started to show up in the form of empty seats. In 2001 the Rams averaged more than 66,000 fans a game. But by 2010, their average home crowd had dropped below 53,000. The losing was certainly a big reason for the decline in attendance. But the team also argued that its

Rams running back Steven Jackson rushed for more than 1,000 yards every season from 2005 to 2012.

RAMS
Rams
39

stadium was outdated and needed to be replaced.

Georgia Frontiere died in 2008, and Stan Kroenke took over ownership of the Rams in 2010. With the attendance problems and stadium issues, some people thought the Rams might move back to Los Angeles. But Kroenke was from Missouri. He promised to keep the team in St. Louis.

Back on the field, the Rams' attempts to find a franchise quarterback continued to fail. The Rams drafted Sam Bradford with the first overall pick in 2010. After going 7–9 his rookie season, Bradford went 1–9 as a starter in 2011. The Rams finished 2–14.

One continued bright spot was running back Steven Jackson. He became the Rams' all-time rushing leader in 2010. He stayed with the team through the 2012 season before leaving to sign with the Atlanta Falcons.

FORGOTTEN QB

Marc Bulger played for the Rams from 2002 to 2009. He ranks second all-time in team passing yards and third in touchdown passes. But he went just 41–54 as a starter. And he went 1–2 in the playoffs. He was not able to continue the success that the team had under Kurt Warner. For that reason, Bulger is sometimes overlooked among all-time great Rams quarterbacks.

Quarterback Sam Bradford, the first overall pick in the 2010 draft, had a hard time staying healthy during his five seasons with the Rams.

That was the same year that veteran head coach Jeff Fisher took over. Fisher knew the Rams well. They had beaten his Tennessee Titans in Super Bowl XXXIV. But Fisher never recorded a winning record in St. Louis.

Todd Gurley rushed for more than 1,000 yards in three of his first four seasons with the Rams.

In fact, no Rams team recorded another winning record in St. Louis. After the Rams and the city could not agree on building a new stadium, Kroenke decided to move the team back to Los Angeles for the 2016 season. Kroenke already owned land in nearby Inglewood, California, and announced plans to build a new stadium. Until it was ready, the team would play at its old home of the Coliseum.

Rams fans in Southern California were thrilled to have their team back. Nearly 90,000 people attended their first preseason game in 2016. That was the biggest crowd ever to watch an NFL preseason game in the United States.

But the Rams did not give fans much to cheer about that first year. With rookie quarterback Jared Goff gaining experience, the Rams scored the fewest points in the NFL and finished 4–12. Fisher was fired in the middle of the season.

The Rams made a bold move in choosing a new coach. They hired the youngest one in modern NFL history. Sean McVay was only 30 years old. He had been the offensive coordinator in Washington. He led an innovative offense that averaged more than 400 yards per game.

McVay turned around the Rams offense as well. In 2017 Goff was one of the league's best quarterbacks. And running back Todd Gurley confirmed his status as a star. He led the NFL in rushing touchdowns and total yards in 2017. The Rams looked like a completely different team when they had the ball. They ended up leading the league in points scored.

The Rams went 11–5 but lost in the first round of the playoffs. Bigger things were expected in 2018. The Rams scored even more points and won even more games. They went 13–3 and won the division again. They beat the Dallas Cowboys for their first playoff victory since January 2005. That set up a matchup against the New Orleans Saints in the conference championship game. A trip to the Super Bowl was on the line.

Tied 20–20 in the final two minutes, the Saints had the ball at the Rams' 13-yard line. They wanted to run the clock down and try a game-winning field goal. But they needed to pick up a first down.

Saints quarterback Drew Brees threw a pass to wide receiver Tommylee Lewis. Just as Lewis reached for the ball, the Rams' Nickell Robey-Coleman knocked him out of the way. It should have been pass interference. But the officials missed the call.

New Orleans had to settle for a field goal. The Rams had enough time to tie the game on their own field goal, and they won it in overtime on kicker Greg Zuerlein's 57-yard field goal. Saints fans were furious. But it was the Rams who got to go to the Super Bowl.

The Rams did not capitalize on their good luck two weeks later in the Super Bowl. The New England Patriots completely

The Patriots kept Jared Goff and the Rams offense bottled up during the Super Bowl.

shut down the Los Angeles offense. The Rams did not even score until the second half. They matched the record for the fewest points by a team in a Super Bowl in their 13–3 loss.

But the future was bright in the Golden State. The Rams had a core of Goff, Gurley, and defensive tackle Aaron Donald. They had an innovative young coach in McVay. And they had a new stadium to look forward to. Fans hoped a championship was just ahead.

TIMELINE

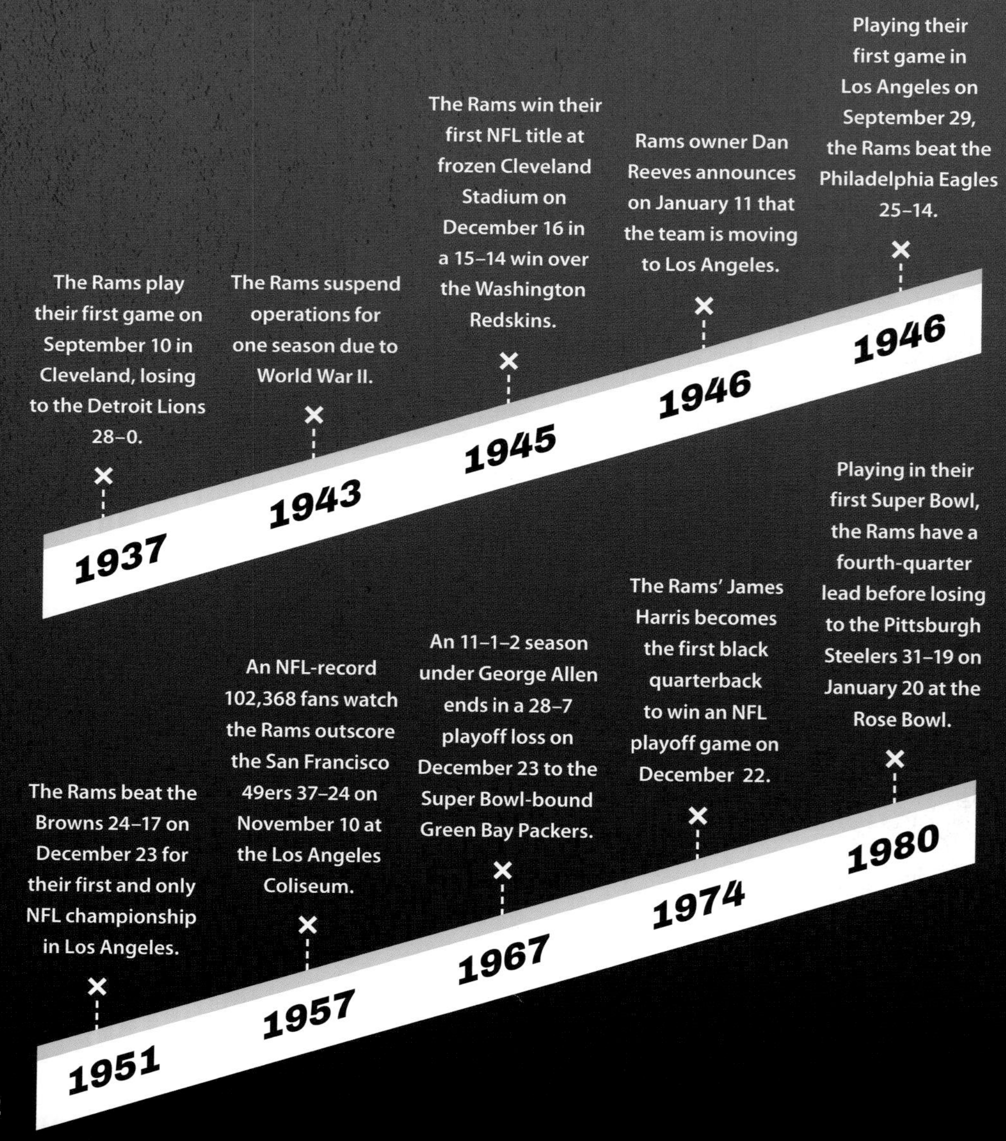

1937
The Rams play their first game on September 10 in Cleveland, losing to the Detroit Lions 28–0.
1943
The Rams suspend operations for one season due to World War II.
1945
The Rams win their first NFL title at frozen Cleveland Stadium on December 16 in a 15–14 win over the Washington Redskins.
1946
Rams owner Dan Reeves announces on January 11 that the team is moving to Los Angeles.
1946
Playing their first game in Los Angeles on September 29, the Rams beat the Philadelphia Eagles 25–14.
1951
The Rams beat the Browns 24–17 on December 23 for their first and only NFL championship in Los Angeles.
1957
An NFL-record 102,368 fans watch the Rams outscore the San Francisco 49ers 37–24 on November 10 at the Los Angeles Coliseum.
1967
An 11–1–2 season under George Allen ends in a 28–7 playoff loss on December 23 to the Super Bowl-bound Green Bay Packers.
1974
The Rams' James Harris becomes the first black quarterback to win an NFL playoff game on December 22.
1980
Playing in their first Super Bowl, the Rams have a fourth-quarter lead before losing to the Pittsburgh Steelers 31–19 on January 20 at the Rose Bowl.

1984
Eric Dickerson breaks O. J. Simpson's NFL season rushing record in a December 9 game against the Houston Oilers at Anaheim Stadium.

1995
St. Louis's second NFL team makes its home debut on September 10 as the Rams beat the New Orleans Saints 17–13 at Busch Stadium.

1995
The Rams open the TWA Dome on November 12 with a 28–17 victory over the Carolina Panthers.

1999
The Rams acquire running back Marshall Faulk on April 15 from the Indianapolis Colts.

2000
The Rams finally win a Super Bowl, 23–16, over the Tennessee Titans January 30 in the Georgia Dome.

2002
In their third Super Bowl, the Rams are edged 20–17 by the New England Patriots on February 3 at the Louisiana Superdome.

2003
Under head coach Mike Martz, the Rams have their last winning season in St. Louis, going 12–4.

2016
After 21 seasons in St. Louis, owner Stan Kroenke announces the team will relocate back to Los Angeles.

2017
The Rams hire 30-year-old Sean McVay as head coach.

2019
After a 13–3 season, the Rams win the NFC and play the New England Patriots in Super Bowl LIII, losing 13–3.

QUICK STATS

FRANCHISE HISTORY

Cleveland Rams 1937–45
Los Angeles Rams 1946–94, 2016–
St. Louis Rams 1995–2015

SUPER BOWLS *(wins in bold)*

1979 (XIV), **1999 (XXXIV)**, 2001 (XXXVI), 2018 (LIII)

NFL CHAMPIONSHIP GAMES *(wins in bold)*

1945, 1949, 1950, **1951**, 1955

NFC CHAMPIONSHIP GAMES *(since 1970 AFL-NFL merger)*

1974, 1975, 1976, 1978, 1979, 1985, 1989, 1999, 2001, 2018

KEY COACHES

George Allen (1966–70): 49–17–4, 0–2 (playoffs)
Chuck Knox (1973–77, 1992–94): 69–48–1, 3–5 (playoffs)
Sean McVay (2017–): 24–8, 2–2 (playoffs)
Dick Vermeil (1997–99): 22–26, 3–0 (playoffs)

KEY PLAYERS *(position, seasons with team)*

Isaac Bruce (WR, 1994–2007)
Eric Dickerson (RB, 1983–87)
Aaron Donald (DT, 2014–)
Jim Everett (QB, 1986–93)
Marshall Faulk (RB, 1999–2005)
Tom Fears (WR, 1948–56)
Elroy "Crazylegs" Hirsch (RB–WR, 1949–57)
Torry Holt (WR, 1999–2008)
Deacon Jones (DE, 1961–71)
Merlin Olsen (DT, 1962–76)
Norm Van Brocklin (QB, 1949–57)
Kurt Warner (QB, 1998–2003)
Bob Waterfield (QB, 1945–52)
Jack Youngblood (DE, 1971–84)

HOME FIELDS

Los Angeles Memorial Coliseum (1946–79, 2016–)
Edward Jones Dome (1995–2015)
Also known as TWA Dome
Busch Stadium (1995)
Anaheim Stadium (1980–94)
League Park (1937, 1942, 1944–45)
Municipal Stadium (1937, 1939–41, 1945)
Shaw Stadium (1938)

*All statistics through 2018 season

QUOTES AND ANECDOTES

The signature rams-horn design on the team's helmets originated with running back Fred Gehrke in 1947. An art major in college, Gehrke painted the yellow horn on a leather helmet. Eventually he painted 70 helmets. The Rams thus became the first pro team to feature a logo on their helmets. Today, only the Cleveland Browns in the NFL lack a helmet logo.

Los Angeles Rams players made the most of their location near Hollywood. Many players ended up having movie and TV acting careers that lasted longer than their time in football. Among the Rams players who also starred in Hollywood were Bob Waterfield, Elroy "Crazylegs" Hirsch, Woody Strode, Bernie Casey, Roosevelt Grier, Merlin Olsen, Fred Dryer, and Roman Gabriel. Hirsch played himself in a 1953 movie *Crazylegs*. Olsen co-starred in the TV series *Little House on the Prairie*, then starred in his own series, *Father Murphy*. Strode, one of the first two black players in the postwar NFL, also was one of the earliest featured black actors starting in the mid-1950s. His most famous role was as John Wayne's sidekick in *The Man Who Shot Liberty Valance* in 1962.

The Rams made Aaron Donald the highest-paid defensive player in NFL history in 2018, but only briefly. They signed the Pro Bowler to a six-year contract extension worth $135 million before the start of the season. But one day later, the Chicago Bears signed linebacker Khalil Mack to a deal worth $141 million.

GLOSSARY

contenders
People or teams that have a good chance at winning a championship.

contract
An agreement to play for a certain team.

draft
A system that allows teams to acquire new players coming into a league.

franchise
A sports organization, including the top-level team and all minor league affiliates.

free agency
A period during which players are free to sign with any team of their choosing after their contract expires.

general manager
A team employee responsible for negotiating contracts with that team's players.

Hall of Fame
The highest honor a player or coach can get when his or her career is over.

integrate
To include people from more than one race.

momentum
The strength or force that allows something to continue or to grow stronger.

retire
To end one's career.

rookie
A professional athlete in his or her first year of competition.

MORE INFORMATION

BOOKS

Cohn, Nate. *Los Angeles Rams*. New York: AV2 by Weigl, 2018.

Lajiness, Katie. *Los Angeles Rams*. Minneapolis, MN: Abdo Publishing, 2017.

McGee, Earl. *Los Angeles Rams*. Minneapolis, MN: Abdo Publishing, 2017.

ONLINE RESOURCES

To learn more the Los Angeles Rams, visit **abdobooklinks.com** or scan this QR code. These links are routinely monitored and updated to provide the most current information available.

PLACE TO VISIT

Pro Football Hall of Fame
2121 George Halas Dr. NW
Canton, OH 44708
330–456–8207
profootballhof.com

This hall of fame and museum highlights the greatest players and moments in the history of the National Football League. Former Rams who have been enshrined include Bob Waterfield, Eric Dickerson, Kurt Warner, and Marshall Faulk.

INDEX

ABOUT THE AUTHOR

William Meier has worked as an author and editor in the publishing industry for more than 25 years. He resides in St. Louis, Missouri, with his wife and their poodle, Macy.